Intersections:
Where Faith and Life Meet

A Cumberland Presbyterian
Adult Resource
Volume 16, Call

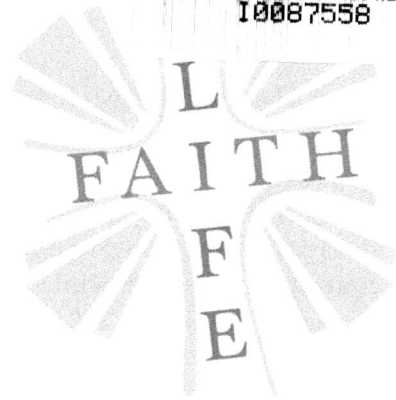

Discipleship Ministry Team
Ministry Council
Cumberland Presbyterian Church

8207 Traditional Place
Cordova, Tennessee 38016

First Edition 2017

Published by The Discipleship Ministry Team
General Assembly Ministry Council of the Cumberland Presbyterian Church
Cordova, Tennessee

ISBN-13: 978-1-945929-05-2
ISBN-10: 1945929057

We want to hear from you.
Please send your comments about this curriculum to
the Discipleship Ministry Team at chm@cumberland.org.

OUR UNITED OUTREACH
Made Possible In Part By Your Tithe To Our United Outreach

Table of Contents

Editor: Cindy Martin
Proofreader: Pam Campbell

To order, call 901-276-4572, x 252 or e-mail resources@cumberland.org.

The Spark that Lit the Burning Bush

Scripture for lesson: Exodus 2:23-25; 3:1-14

Whom do you know who has made a difference because he or she answered God's call?

Whom do you know who has given his or her time to make the world a better place? How can you help to make the world a better place?

With three daughters, our family life can become so busy it feels as if we are frantically running on a spinning gerbil wheel. During the school year, all my daughters take dance lessons, which occupy Tuesday and Wednesday evenings. So when my wife said the dance school would be starting a new class on Friday evenings and the girls wanted to participate, I immediately tried to put my foot down. My wife explained that our daughters were not going to be students, but "buddies." Huh?

A few years ago a lady named Judy Mayberry had three daughters, the youngest of whom was born with spina bifida and needed a wheelchair. When Judy's two older daughters took dance lessons, her youngest daughter did not understand why she could not participate. Emotionally moved and heartbroken for her child, Judy formed "I Can Dance of Arkansas," based on Philippians 4:13, "I can do all things through him [Christ] who strengthens me." "I Can" is a free program that gives children who have physical challenges the opportunity to be a part of a dance class. This class relies on "buddies"—children who know how to dance—to help teach the students with special challenges.

My protests of not wanting to add something else to our schedule dissolved. I knew that this class would be the most important one in which my children would ever participate. "I Can" has changed the lives of so many children—those who have physical challenges and those with none—and it has changed the lives of every parent who has a child involved. One woman answered God's call to make a difference in people's lives. The world is a better place because she answered that call.

Prep for the Journey

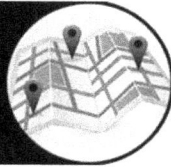

As the Book of Exodus opens, hundreds of thousands of God's people are enslaved in Egypt. These slaves were the descendants of Abraham, with whom God had established the covenant to father a great people—those who would be known as God's people. Abraham's descendants were Isaac, Jacob, and Joseph, who had become second only to Pharaoh as a ruler in Egypt.

Joseph foretold the coming of a great famine, thus allowing the Egyptians to set aside storehouses of food. The famine also hit the land of Canaan, where Jacob and the rest of his family lived. Because food was available in Egypt, Joseph's family relocated there. After Joseph's death, the descendants of Jacob continued to live in Egypt for many generations. As long as people remembered Joseph and his contribution to their country, his family was safe. However, the Hebrew people, as they were called, eventually became so numerous that the Egyptians were afraid that they might try to take over the country.

The Egyptian pharaoh decided the only way to control the Hebrew people was to make slaves of them. Despite their suffering, the Hebrew people continued to thrive and multiply. In an effort to control the population explosion, Pharaoh decreed that all male babies born to Hebrew women were to be killed. Surely God would answer their cries; surely God would do something.

When have you relocated? How have you sensed God using you in the new location?

What things enslave people today? How can we seek freedom from those things?

On the Road

Read Exodus 2:23-25.

After a long time the king of Egypt died. The Israelites groaned under their slavery, and cried out. Out of the slavery their cry for help rose up to God. ²⁴ God heard their groaning, and God remembered his covenant with Abraham, Isaac, and Jacob. ²⁵ God looked upon the Israelites, and God took notice of them.

The question, "Does God care?" has crossed the lips of many people who are enduring difficult situations. At times we have all felt abandoned or ignored. Exodus 12:40 tells us that the children of Israel lived in Egypt for 430 years. We don't know how much of that time was spent in slavery, but that was a long time of crying to God for help. Some of them probably thought, "Is God listening?"

When have you cried out to God and wondered if God were listening? How do you listen for God?

When have you reflected on situations and seen God at work in those circumstances?

When have you become upset because of an injustice you witnessed? Explain.

When have you experienced a place that felt like holy ground to you? What caused those feelings?

How does God get your attention? How do you know that God is involved?

Despite what might have appeared as God's indifference to the people, God was preparing a way to save them. An Egyptian princess had rescued a Hebrew baby when she found him floating in a basket along the river's edge. Adopting him as her son, he was given the full benefit of being raised in the royal household. However, because his own mother was allowed to care for him when he was young, this boy also grew up knowing that he was a Hebrew, which also meant that he knew of his people's special relationship with God. This boy's name was Moses.

Read Exodus 3:1-6.

Moses was keeping the flock of his father-in-law Jethro, the priest of Midian; he led his flock beyond the wilderness, and came to Horeb, the mountain of God. ² There the angel of the LORD appeared to him in a flame of fire out of a bush; he looked, and the bush was blazing, yet it was not consumed. ³ Then Moses said, "I must turn aside and look at this great sight, and see why the bush is not burned up." ⁴ When the LORD saw that he had turned aside to see, God called to him out of the bush, "Moses, Moses!" And he said, "Here I am." ⁵ Then he said, "Come no closer! Remove the sandals from your feet, for the place on which you are standing is holy ground." ⁶ He said further, "I am the God of your father, the God of Abraham, the God of Isaac, and the God of Jacob." And Moses hid his face, for he was afraid to look at God.

Moses had fled from Egypt after killing an Egyptian who was beating a Hebrew slave, one of Moses' own relatives. Moses settled in the land of Midian and tended his father-in-law's sheep. He came across an odd scene: a bush that was on fire, but was not being consumed by the fire. Approaching the bush, Moses was told to remove his sandals because he was standing on holy ground. In some cultures and religions, the custom of removing ones shoes or sandals before entering a holy place continues to be a sign of reverence and respect. Removing his shoes may also have been an indication that Moses was to remain for some time in the presence of God. He was invited to enter into a place that was better than anything he had seen before.

Remember that Moses lived during a time when many cultures worshiped multiple gods. The idea of one God was unique to the Hebrews. It makes sense, then, that God mentions Abraham, Isaac, and Jacob as a way of establishing a connection with Moses. Their names would have been as familiar to Moses and the Hebrew people as George Washington, Thomas Jefferson, and Benjamin Franklin are to people of the United States. By saying, "I am the God of your father, the God of Abraham, the God of Isaac, and the God of Jacob," God immediately garnered Moses' complete attention.

Read Exodus 3:7-14.

Then the LORD said, "I have observed the misery of my people who are in Egypt; I have heard their cry on account of their taskmasters. Indeed, I know their sufferings, ⁸ and I have come down to deliver them from the Egyptians, and to bring them up out of that land to a good and broad land, a land flowing with milk and honey, to the country of the Canaanites, the Hittites, the Amorites, the Perizzites, the Hivites, and the Jebusites. ⁹ The cry of the Israelites has now come to me; I have also seen how the Egyptians oppress them. ¹⁰ So come, I will send you to Pharaoh to bring my people, the Israelites, out of Egypt." ¹¹ But Moses said to God, "Who am I that I should go to Pharaoh, and bring the Israelites out of Egypt?" ¹² He said, "I will be with you; and this shall be the sign for you that it is I who sent you: when you have brought the people out of Egypt, you shall worship God on this mountain."

¹³ But Moses said to God, "If I come to the Israelites and say to them, 'The God of your ancestors has sent me to you,' and they ask me, 'What is his name?' what shall I say to them?" ¹⁴ God said to Moses, "I AM WHO I AM." He said further, "Thus you shall say to the Israelites, 'I AM has sent me to you.'"

When asked the name of God, the response was quite simple—or perhaps it was quite complicated. How do you actually put a name on the Creator of the universe? How do you put a name on the beginning and the end? God has always been and always will be. People are born and people die, yet God is still there. War and peace come and go, and God is still there. The seasons change as does the world, and God is still there. There is pain and suffering and celebration of life, and God is still there. I AM present, I AM with you, I AM life, I AM love, I AM forgiveness. The best way to describe the all-present God in our lives: "I AM."

Scenic Route

Moses was hesitant to accept God's call, offering multiple excuses as to why God should choose someone else. Recall that Moses had not left Egypt under the best circumstances. In fact, he was a fugitive wanted for murder! So, when God told Moses, "I will send you to Pharaoh to bring my people out of Egypt," Moses' first thought had to have been, "I am the worst possible person you can send; I am wanted for murder in Egypt and can't even risk entering the country." I am sure Moses was thinking, "God if you want this thing to work, you have the wrong person for the job!"

God was looking at things from a different perspective. While Moses thought he was the wrong person for the job, God knew that Moses was exactly the right choice. God needed someone who could relate to the Hebrew slaves and to the rulers. Moses had spent a significant amount of time with both groups, making him the perfect person to negotiate the slaves' freedom.

How do you "name" God to someone who is unfamiliar with the concept of one God?

When have you recognized God's presence in your life? How do you identify God's presence?

What things in your life do you see as hindrances to serving God? How might God be able to use even those things?

When have you found your perspective to be different from God's? What happened?

There was something else that made Moses the perfect candidate to lead the Hebrews out of slavery. Moses had compassion for his fellow Hebrews who were enduring pain and suffering. God also felt compassion for the Hebrew people, which was the spark that lit the burning bush.

Workers Ahead — CAUTION

God is looking for obedient servants to make the world a better place, which is the basis of God's calling in our lives. So many times we are like Moses, looking at what we see as limitations rather than trusting God to use us as we are. Do we really think God would call us to something we were incapable of doing?

Many people have come to me with the burning concern, "I don't know what I am supposed to do with my life." Maybe the first thing we should do in response to that pondering is to identify those issues about which we are passionate. Those burning passions inside might be our own burning bushes. Theologian Frederick Buechner suggests that calling is where the deep gladness of your heart meets the world's great need. The passion burning inside of us is something that didn't just happen; it was put there by I AM. The same I AM who told Moses, "I will be with you." Every calling of God comes with a promise, I AM with you. You will never be alone.

There are so many injustices in our world that it is easy to feel overwhelmed by all the needs. We may want to help those who are hungry, homeless, grieving, sick, depressed, struggling financially or emotionally,…and the list continues. We can't do it all, but when we respond to the passionate call that God has put on our hearts, we can make a difference. In addition to focusing our efforts on our passions, we can and should contribute to a local food or clothing drive or offer words of love and encouragement when they are needed.

Where is God leading you at this time in your life? How are you uniquely equipped to respond to that call?

What does the name "I AM" mean to you?

Where do you feel the most passionate about serving? How might your group serve together?

In the Rear View

Moses seems to have been content tending his father-in-law's sheep. It is easy for us to get into a routine, doing the same thing day after day. Getting used to routines makes it more difficult to see the disturbances of God in our lives that call us to something new and different. We can also become resistant to God's call because it involves change, which is something that many humans find difficult!

People are continuing to cry out to God. Some of those people we know personally. God is still lighting bushes in our lives and in our hearts to get our attention. God wants us to join in the work of offering comfort and hope to those who are suffering. Think back to the "I Can" story at the beginning of this lesson. Where do you need to start a new dance class?

Which of your routines needs to be disrupted? Why?

Who in your life is crying out? How is God calling you to offer comfort and hope to them?

Travel Log

Day 1:

There are times when we have cried out to God, becoming discouraged because it seemed that there were no answers to our prayers. Sometimes weeks, months, or years pass before we are able to look back and see how God worked in a particular situation. When have you cried out to God, not knowing how you would survive a difficult time? How were you able to recognize God in those times? Journal your thoughts.

Day 2:

Most Christians wonder what God is calling them to do. While we may feel as if we have identified that calling at some point, we must also remember that God's calling may change throughout a person's life. List those things about which you are passionate. Then identify things you enjoy doing. How can you use the things you enjoy doing to serve God in the areas about which you are passionate? (For instance: If someone likes to hunt or fish, the meat or the catch could be donated to help feed people who are hungry. Or, someone who enjoys knitting or crocheting could make blankets or hats for people who are living on the streets.)

Day 3:

Sometimes our daily routine prevents us from seeing God around us. Write down your daily schedule, the places you go, the people you see, etc. As you reflect on your routine, where might you be missing God? How can you make yourself more aware of God in your everyday routines?

Day 4:

When Moses asked God's name, God responded, "I AM." I AM can mean a lot of different things. What does I AM mean to you? Write the words I AM several times in a column. Then go through and fill in behind each I AM a word or a phrase of who you need God to be to you at this moment in your life. (For example: I AM love, I AM comfort.)

Day 5:

Moses' people needed help. Who are "your people"? Think about the people with whom you work, those who live in your community, those in your church, and so forth. List each of these groups or individuals and then pray for them. Consider how you can make a positive difference in the lives of those around you.

Day 6:

Again think of the people with whom you are in contact every day. Write down some of the needs that you know these people have. Pray for each person/group. Ask God to show you how you can help meet those needs.

Day 7:

God is looking for people to bring peace and hope in the world. While God calls us to help those in need, there are also others whom God sends to us when we are in need. Think of some people in your life who you know God has sent. Write a prayer of thanks for these people and how they represented God to you in a specific situation.

It's not just about Appearances

Scripture for Lesson: 1 Samuel 15:24-26; 15:34–16:1-13

When have you suspected that someone was deceiving you? How did his or her actions make you feel?

In our family, birthdays are a big deal. We always have birthday parties for our children and invite their friends to make the day special. We also have a celebration with just our family of five, and the honoree chooses the restaurant where we will have a meal together. As my 40th birthday approached, I knew my family was planning something a little extra because there was way too much whispering, and I caught parts of too many conversations happening behind my back. So I decided to have a little fun.

A few weeks earlier, my daughters had been asking me where I wanted to eat for my birthday. I told them I had plenty of time to decide. "No, Dad, we need to know now," they insisted.

Finally I told them I wanted to go to my favorite crawfish and shrimp boiling house.

A few days before my birthday, I told them I had changed my mind. Instead of going out to eat, I said I would really like just to stay home and eat at our house as a family.

My children adamantly protested. "Daddy, we have to go out to eat for your birthday; it's tradition!"

"Are you girls planning something I don't know about?" I asked repeatedly.

The answer was always an emphatic, "No!"

When my birthday arrived, my wife spent a lot of time texting, and the children were antsy. That evening we headed out to dinner at a time chosen by my family, not by me. Once we got to the restaurant, my children insisted that I walk in first.

"Why do I need to walk in first? Is there something going on I don't know about?"

"No, Daddy, just go in."

Once inside the restaurant, we were escorted to the back room where my mother, brother, nieces, nephew, and other friends and family from out of town were waiting. It was the first surprise party I have ever had. While I wasn't actually surprised, I was delighted by the look on the children's faces, thinking they had pulled a fast one on me. The moment was priceless.

At the end of the party, my middle child crawled up in my lap with a sad look on her face. "What's wrong," I asked.

"Daddy, I'm sorry I lied to you. I just thought I had to lie to do what was best."

While I never want to encourage my children to lie, I told her she had done the right thing for the situation and that I wasn't mad at her. What a conundrum! To lie or not to lie.

Prep for the Journey

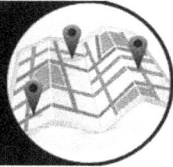

We don't like to associate lies and deceit with the Bible, but many of its stories are filled with trickery and dishonesty. From a very young age, my parents taught me that lying is wrong. If you polled Christians, I believe the overwhelming majority would agree, but in the scripture for this lesson, God told Samuel to lie and deceive.

From the time Israel became a nation after leaving Egypt, it had been ruled by tribal elders and judges with the understanding that God was their king. However, the people eventually decided they wanted an earthly king like those of other nations. Samuel was serving as the judge at that time, and neither God nor Samuel was pleased with the people's desire for a human king. Samuel warned the people that a human king would take their sons to serve in his armies and their daughters to work in his kitchens. An earthly king would also take the best of their harvests. Yet they persisted in their demand.

God told Samuel, "They have not rejected you, but they have rejected me" (1 Samuel 8:7b). God relented and sent Samuel to find a king.

Meanwhile, Saul, a young man from the tribe of Benjamin, was looking for his father's donkeys. He had traveled quite a distance in search of the animals when his servant boy realized they were close to where a man of God was known to live. Thinking that this man of God, Samuel, might be able to help them locate the donkeys, Saul and his friend went in search of him. Samuel was on his way to bless a sacrifice before joining a feast when he encountered Saul.

Samuel realized Saul was the king he had been sent to find. The scripture tells us, "There was not a man among the people of Israel more handsome than he; he stood head and shoulders above everyone else" (1 Samuel 9:2b). We might be tempted to think that Samuel saw this striking young man and took it upon himself to choose the king, but Samuel sought God's guidance in this important decision. God had revealed to Samuel that he would meet the future king during his travels and confirmed that the identity of the king would be clear. Samuel invited Saul to join the feast and gave him the seat

When have you found deception necessary? How did you feel about using deception? How do you react when someone lies to or deceives you? How does the intention or the situation affect the way you feel about the deception?

How do you feel about the Bible containing stories of trickery and dishonesty? about God using lies and deceit to accomplish God's purposes?

When have you wanted something despite having been advised against it? Why did you want it? If you received it, what happened? How did you feel?

How does appearance affect your choice of leaders? How likely are you to seek God's guidance when choosing a leader?

When have you had to remain quiet about exciting news? How did you handle the situation?

When have you unexpectedly been chosen for a role of importance? What happened?

How can human views get in the way of God's will? When have you found yourself guilty of getting in the way of God's will?

of honor. Naturally, Saul was quite confused by Samuel's actions, and soon things became even stranger.

When the feast was over, Samuel anointed Saul as ruler over the people of Israel. He gave Saul very specific instructions, including that he was to wait for seven days after returning home until Samuel would come to give him further directions. Saul did not tell anyone about being anointed king.

Samuel called all of the tribes of Israel together and had the people come forward by tribe and then by each family within the tribe. When Saul's family was called, he could not be found because he had hidden among the baggage! When he was found and brought forward, Samuel announced him as the king God had chosen for the people of Israel. He looked the part and had the support of the people.

On the Road

Soon after becoming king, Saul began to think that he could handle things without God and began to disobey. While Saul might have looked like a king, his heart was focused on selfish ambitions. God knew what was in Saul's heart, and when Saul repeatedly ignored God, things had to change. Samuel was tasked with telling Saul that God had rejected him as king.

Read 1 Samuel 15:24-26.

Saul said to Samuel, "I have sinned; for I have transgressed the commandment of the LORD and your words, because I feared the people and obeyed their voice. [25] Now therefore, I pray, pardon my sin, and return with me, so that I may worship the LORD." [26] Samuel said to Saul, "I will not return with you; for you have rejected the word of the LORD, and the LORD has rejected you from being king over Israel."

Instead of seeking God's guidance for the decisions he had to make, Saul had listened to the people and made decisions based on what they wanted. He fell into the trap of being more concerned about others' opinions than doing what was righteous in the eyes of God.

Read 1 Samuel 15:34–16:1.

Then Samuel went to Ramah; and Saul went up to his house in Gibeah of Saul. [35] Samuel did not see Saul again until the day of his death, but Samuel grieved over Saul. And the LORD was sorry that he had made Saul king over Israel.

[16] The LORD said to Samuel, "How long will you grieve over Saul? I have rejected him from being king over Israel. Fill your horn with oil

When have you had to break bad news to someone? How did you approach the situation?

and set out; I will send you to Jesse the Bethlehemite, for I have provided for myself a king among his sons."

Evidently Samuel grieved over Saul for quite a while. In fact, God scolded Samuel, in essence telling him to get over it and move on. We don't know why Samuel grieved for Saul. Maybe Samuel really liked Saul, despite his imperfections. It is difficult to see friends or loved ones make mistakes that can lead them down a dark road. Even though they may make unwise decisions, we are still saddened by the circumstances and are concerned for them. Regardless of the reason for Samuel's grief, God was calling him to separate himself from that situation and to find a king who was best for the people.

Read 1 Samuel 16:2-5.

Samuel said, "How can I go? If Saul hears of it, he will kill me." And the LORD said, "Take a heifer with you, and say, 'I have come to sacrifice to the LORD.' ³ Invite Jesse to the sacrifice, and I will show you what you shall do; and you shall anoint for me the one whom I name to you." ⁴ Samuel did what the LORD commanded, and came to Bethlehem. The elders of the city came to meet him trembling, and said, "Do you come peaceably?" ⁵ He said, "Peaceably; I have come to sacrifice to the LORD; sanctify yourselves and come with me to the sacrifice." And he sanctified Jesse and his sons and invited them to the sacrifice.

Samuel had to be very careful. Saul still saw himself as king, and so did the people of Israel. Samuel knew that anointing someone else as king would be considered an act of treason, punishable by death. When God told Samuel to go to Bethlehem and anoint a new king, Samuel was understandably hesitant.

When Samuel expressed his concern, God told him to go to Bethlehem to offer a sacrifice, which gave his trip a legitimate, and safe, purpose. God told Samuel the next king would be one of the sons of Jesse. While in Bethlehem, Samuel invited Jesse and his sons to the sacrifice, which gave him an opportunity to anoint the future king.

Read 1 Samuel 16:6-13.

When they came, he looked on Eliab and thought, "Surely the LORD's anointed is now before the LORD." ⁷ But the LORD said to Samuel, "Do not look on his appearance or on the height of his stature, because I have rejected him; for the LORD does not see as mortals see; they look on the outward appearance, but the LORD looks on the heart." ⁸ Then Jesse called Abinadab, and made him pass before Samuel. He said, "Neither has the LORD chosen this one." ⁹ Then Jesse made Shammah pass by. And he said, "Neither has the LORD chosen this one." ¹⁰ Jesse made seven of his sons pass before Samuel, and Samuel said to Jesse, "The LORD has not chosen any of these." ¹¹ Samuel said to Jesse, "Are all your sons here?" And he said, "There remains yet the youngest, but he is keeping the sheep." And Samuel said to Jesse, "Send and bring him; for we will not sit down until he comes here." ¹² He sent and brought him in. Now he was ruddy, and had beautiful eyes, and was handsome. The LORD said,

Why might Samuel have grieved so for Saul? When have you grieved about a situation that was of a person's own making? When have you succumbed to the trap of listening to others rather than doing what you knew was right?

How would you feel about facing dangerous circumstances to carry out God's command?

When have you become aware that a person's outward appearance belied what was in his or her heart?

"Rise and anoint him; for this is the one." [13] *Then Samuel took the horn of oil, and anointed him in the presence of his brothers; and the spirit of the LORD came mightily upon David from that day forward. Samuel then set out and went to Ramah.*

We can imagine the scenario: God's representative specifically invited Jesse and his sons to join him in offering a sacrifice to God. That would likely have seemed odd, but then each of the sons had to pass before this holy man, being sanctified. They must have wondered what was going on, especially when Samuel asked if Jesse had any more sons. The youngest son was with the sheep. According to the laws of cleanliness, David would have had to purify himself before being able to attend the sacrifice. Yet Samuel stated that they would not begin until this youngest son was present.

While Saul had looked very "kingly," David was only a boy. Nevertheless, God was calling David to be the next king of Israel. If Samuel had any doubts, God reminded him that despite Saul's apparent outward suitability to be king, he had not followed God's will. Rather than considering outward appearances, God was looking at what was in David's heart.

Scenic Route

By cross-referencing some of the psalms that David wrote, especially 51 and 69, scholars have pieced together information about David's early life. Based on David's own comments, it is possible that his parentage was questionable. Some think that Jesse, David's father, had concerns about the purity of his own lineage because of the edict against marrying a Moabite. Ruth, Jesse's grandmother, was a Moabite convert to Judaism. The logic behind this theory becomes very complicated as it involves ancient sanctions and possible deceit by David's mother.

A more "traditional" explanation for David's supposed illegitimacy is that his mother had an extra-marital affair. If this was indeed the case, she would have brought shame upon the entire family and the resulting offspring would have been shunned even within the family. Both of the above mentioned psalms contain references to David's alienation, especially from his brothers. They may even have been responsible for David's initial exclusion from the meeting with Samuel.

Just imagine the brothers' surprise and probable chagrin when Samuel insisted that David be called from the fields to join them in the sacrifice! We can only guess at their reaction when he became king.

When have you suffered alienation? Who helped to restore you to right relationships? How did those who had shunned you react when this person intervened on your behalf?

Workers Ahead

Corrie ten Boom and her family lived in Amsterdam during World War II. When Holland was occupied by the Nazis, the ten Boom family felt called to protect those whom the Nazis were persecuting, especially people of the Jewish faith. They built a special hiding place by creating a false wall in Corrie's bedroom. This small room would hold six people, all of whom had to stand while in it.

Unfortunately, word spread among the community and a fellow citizen turned them in to the Gestapo. The ten Boom family was sent to concentration camps. Corrie was the only one to survive. She was inexplicably released from the camp about a week before all of the women her age were executed.

Although the situation was extremely dangerous for the ten Boom family, they did not hesitate to do what they felt was right. Corrie once said that for her the most difficult part of her family's efforts were the necessary lies.

The ten Boom family did not have any special training for the situation in which they found themselves, but their efforts helped to save the lives of approximately 800 Jews. They loved God and followed God's calling to love all people, even to the point of death.

People today willingly go into dangerous situations when God calls them. It is hard for many Christians who live in the United States to identify with people who answer God's call to serve in places where they could be killed for their beliefs. These people sacrifice their safety and the comforts of home and family to go where God has called them. Where is God calling you?

In the Rear View

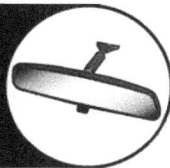

Some people will read this story from First Samuel and label it the calling of David, but I see it as the calling of Samuel. God called Samuel to defy the king, risk his life, and anoint a new king. Samuel put himself in harm's way to do what God was calling him to do.

While God's call for our lives might not put us in harm's way, it could lead us down unpopular paths. Following God's call can even damage relationships with friends and family and create problems in business dealings. God knows what is best for all of us. We should continue to search our hearts for God's will instead of following the desires of the world.

To what extent would you risk yourself and/or your family to do what you felt was right?

Whom is God calling you to love? How willing are you to accept God's call?

When have you struggled to make the right decision because you knew that your response would not be popular?

Travel Log

Day 1:

At some point in everyone's life, he or she will have to make a difficult decision, one that may well be unpopular. When have you faced tough decisions? How did you make the decision? What was the outcome? Journal your thoughts about how you followed God's call and leading in making these decisions. Include a few of the good things that eventually came about after making these decisions.

Day 2:

Many people in our world live in extremely dangerous situations. In some of these situations, people must deceive others simply to stay alive. Who are some of these people? What are their situations? Write down some words of encouragement for people in such situations and then pray for them. If you know of a safe way to send words of encouragement to missionaries or others who are serving in dangerous circumstances, send a note.

Day 3:

"For the LORD does not see as mortals see; they look on the outward appearance, but the LORD looks on the heart." In what situations are you aware of people being judged solely on the basis of their outward appearances? Whom have you unfairly judged? How can you correct this wrong? Make a few notes as to what can happen when we fail to look at a person's heart.

Day 4:

The ultimate call of God is to love our neighbor. Make a list of specific ways you can show love to others. Employ some of those ideas beginning today.

Day 5:

We cannot serve two masters. Sometimes the popular ways of the world can prevent us from caring about those around us. What are some things that hinder you from loving and caring about others? Record your hindrances and then list some ways of freeing yourself from those things.

Day 6:

David was a youth in whom God saw tremendous potential. Consider the young people in your life. What potential do you see in them? How can you help them develop that potential? Write several young people notes (or send emails or texts) that tell them the gifts you see and how God might be calling them to use those gifts.

Day 7:

God sent Samuel to anoint David because removing Saul as king would ultimately be best for the people. Yet it took several years before Saul was actually off the throne. During that time, David was exposed to life in the royal household and developed leadership experience. When have you had to wait for God's timing? How does this story encourage you today? Jot down a few thoughts.

Great Expectations

Scripture for lesson: Jeremiah 1:4-9

FAITH LIFE

How do you often respond when faced with a day when nothing seems to be going as planned?

When have you been in a frustrating situation only to discover you were exactly where God needed you?

It was early Wednesday morning and everyone in our family was getting ready for the day. Wednesdays are extremely busy and often long days. My wife was running late for work, so despite needing to be at the church early, I offered to drop off our children at school. As I was hurrying back to the church, my tire went flat. This day was not turning out as I had expected. Finding a parking lot, I pulled over so that I could change the tire safely. After spending time finding the jack and struggling to extract the spare time from under my truck, I was ready for the job. Just as I was about to remove the flat tire, an elderly man approached me.

"You need some help?" he asked.

I responded, "No, thanks. I think I've got it." He didn't take no for an answer and began to give me advice. Apparently he used to own a tire repair shop, "back in the day" and thought I was not doing the job properly.

"You need to jack the front end up a little more before you remove the tire. That tire iron ain't worth a flip. I got one in my truck that is better than that one if you want to use it."

"No thanks. This one is fine."

I was in a hurry. I had plans and places to be and was already behind. This guy was getting in the way. Even though he was getting on my last nerve, I kept my cool. When I had removed the flat and was getting ready to put on the spare tire, the man asked, "Are you here for treatment?"

"Huh?"

When I looked around, I noticed that I had pulled into the parking lot of the Cancer Treatment Center. "No sir. I just happened to limp in here to change my tire. I didn't even realize where I was."

"Yeah, I got treatment first thing in the morning. What a way to start your day. When I got cancer, I had to sell my business and quit work."

I thought a minute and said, "Have you got that other tire iron? You're right—this one ain't worth a flip."

"I'll get it right now." He bossed me through the entire process of putting on my tire and loved every minute of it. Did he help me? Not really. Actually, he got in the way and put me a little further behind schedule. But I knew that I was exactly were God wanted me to be.

Prep for the Journey

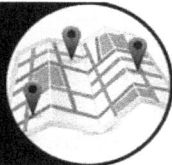

The prophet Jeremiah became one of the most dominant figures of the Old Testament, though he was ridiculed and persecuted by his own people. He received God's call early in life, probably during his early twenties. Chapter 1 of the Book of Jeremiah indicates that the prophet was consecrated—set apart for service—before he was ever born. All we know specifically is that Jeremiah began to prophesy during the reign of King Josiah, who is remembered for his religious reforms.

The Book of Jeremiah never specifically mentions King Josiah, but many scholars believe that Jeremiah traveled to villages throughout Judah, calling the people to accept and implement the reforms that Josiah had instituted. Jeremiah eventually "became disillusioned, seeing that the reformers dealt only with externals rather than with the inner spirit and moral behavior of the people" (*The Interpreter's Bible, Vol. 5*, © 1956, page 779).

Jeremiah's call was not an easy one. He frequently found himself in conflict with the priests and other religious and political leaders, including members of his own family. The people did not want to hear that God was going to pronounce judgment on them because they had stopped following God's ways.

On the Road

The opening verses of Jeremiah answer the question, "Does God have a purpose for my life?" God creates us all with a purpose. Our Creator has placed a calling deep inside the spirit of each person. Jeremiah's calling was to speak God's word to the people.

Read Jeremiah 1:4-5.

Now the word of the LORD came to me saying,
⁵ "Before I formed you in the womb I knew you,
and before you were born I consecrated you;
I appointed you a prophet to the nations."

What does being consecrated mean to you? For what have you been consecrated?

When have you felt God calling you to do something that would put you at odds with family and/or friends? How did you respond?

How did you discover your calling? Who helped you?

What gets in your way of responding to God's call?

What excuses do you give when God calls you to do something? How have you experienced God filling the void of your short-comings and inexperience?

When have you felt as if something was your destiny? How was this call related to a necessity? How was your call confirmed?

How would your speech change if every word you uttered was spoken as if you were God's mouthpiece?

I cannot imagine how Jeremiah felt upon hearing these words from God. Here he was, a boy, but God was calling him to be a prophet. Jeremiah was not alone in his feelings of inadequacy. Moses believed no one would listen to him. Gideon told God that he was poor and insignificant. Jonah ran in the opposite direction.

Read Jeremiah 1:6-9.

Then I said, "Ah, Lord GOD! Truly I do not know how to speak, for I am only a boy." [7] But the LORD said to me,
"Do not say, 'I am only a boy';
for you shall go to all to whom I send you,
and you shall speak whatever I command you.
[8] Do not be afraid of them,
for I am with you to deliver you,
says the LORD."
[9] Then the LORD put out his hand and touched my mouth; and the LORD said to me,
"Now I have put my words in your mouth.

Jeremiah felt that his age and inability to speak eloquently would keep him from doing what God was asking. Yet, perhaps more than any other prophet, he also felt a very strong sense of God's call.

Jeremiah seems to have felt that accepting God's call was his destiny. "Everything brought him to this moment of consciousness, and everything in the years which follow confirms it as 'the will of God'" (*Ibid*, page 800). When calling someone to a task or purpose, God makes it possible for the individual to carry out that call: "I will send you"; "you shall speak what I command"; "I am with you to deliver you."

Jeremiah tells us that God touched his mouth and said, "I have put my words in your mouth." What a powerful image! Jeremiah was to be God's literal mouthpiece. Just imagine the responsibility that Jeremiah undoubtedly felt!

Scenic Route

Jeremiah is often referred to as "the weeping prophet." God had given him a heavy message for the people: Change, or suffer the consequences of your disobedience. When the people refused to change, Jeremiah wept because he knew how devastating the consequences would be. He wept for God's people and the suffering that was sure to come.

Some people get the idea that following God guarantees their lives will be happy and easy. The reality is that the path God puts before us will have ups and downs, pain and celebration. The call of God led Jesus to the cross, and Jesus warned his disciples that following him involves picking up that cross ourselves.

Perhaps no person in the Bible is a better example of being beaten down by pain and sorrow as a result of accepting God's call than Jeremiah. He loathed his calling, which seems to have been a burden throughout his life. But, upon closer examination, we see that Jeremiah had expectations. He became upset because the people to whom he had taken God's word would not listen. Their lack of response frustrated the prophet.

Jeremiah expected a change in the people's behavior and became frustrated when they did not repent. That frustration led to sadness and sorrow. But we must remember that God did not call Jeremiah to get results, and God never told Jeremiah to have expectations. God simply called Jeremiah to take a message to the people. The results were up to God. Jeremiah was simply the messenger. Like the prophet, we would do well to remember that God is in the results business.

Workers Ahead

The idea of being called by God is troubling to some people. God created each of us with a purpose in mind, and we are to seek out that purpose. Sometimes we hear and/or respond to God's call because we become aware of a need. God doesn't call us and then step aside, expecting us to develop a plan or to move forward by ourselves. God calls, equips, leads, and provides. Just as God did with Jeremiah, God will fill the void of our shortcomings and inexperience.

For some people, their calling seems to be obvious, but others struggle to know what God is directing them to do. An elderly friend of mine claims that her purpose was to be a mother to her son, whom she and her husband adopted. Maybe we are fulfilling our call without even realizing it.

At times we can see how God is calling another person, even when that person may be unaware of or struggling to discern God's will. We also may be called to new purposes along our faith journeys. For instance, in a sermon I heard recently, the minister told about her mother feeling called to start a phone ministry. Her mother had never been one who enjoyed talking on the phone, but she is now calling people to check on them and let them know that she is thinking about and praying for them. This new calling is a blessing to her and to those whom she calls. At a different stage of her life, she would not have been as likely to hear and accept that purpose for her life.

How would your life be different if you dropped your expectations of people? of your church? of God?

When have you become frustrated about your lack of results when working for God? How does the interpretation suggested in the text help you to put your efforts in perspective?

In what ways might you be living out God's call for your life? How do you feel about the idea of fulfilling God's call without being aware of doing so?

How has your understanding of God's call for your life changed? When have you helped another person identify his or her calling?

Often we have difficulty understanding God's purpose for our life because we can't see the whole picture. We have to trust God to take care of the details and serve where God leads us, putting aside our own limited expectations and plans. As long as we continue to seek God's will, we will discover what God wants us to do.

In the Rear View

Stuck in that parking lot changing a tire, I was frustrated and upset. "God, why? I have places to be and things I need to be doing." My expectations of how that day was supposed to go were not being met, but when I was able to set aside my expectations, I was able to see that God needed me exactly where I was.

Being attentive to the way God is revealed around us and among us is part of the way we recognize our call. God's work is done by everyday people...every day. It is the small things, the subtle smile or kind word that can impact a person's life and show him or her the love of God. Though we may be called to serve God in a variety of ways, we all share the calling to show the love of God to every person, every day.

When have your plans not aligned with God's plans? In what unexpected places or times have you seen God?

With whom is God calling you to share a message of hope—or repentance? How will you honor that calling?

Travel Log

Day 1:

   Recall a time when you experienced a detour in your plans and later realized you were where God needed you to be. Describe how you felt at the time by writing a few descriptive words or by sketching some images. Then add how your feelings changed as you realized how God was using you in that situation.

Day 2:

   Jeremiah faced difficult circumstances for most of his life. He was ostracized by his own people, yet he continued to follow God's call. How do you react to difficult circumstances? Write down your responses. Contemplate how you might deal with these times more effectively. Look back at your comments in a few days to see how well you have employed your ideas.

Day 3:

Find an area where you can spend a few minutes without distractions. Contemplate how God may be calling you. What excuses are you using to avoid responding to God's call? Journal your thoughts as you spend time in discernment of God's will for your life.

Day 4:

Reflect about your day. Where have you seen God today? Record the people and situations where God was revealed. How did those people and situations help you to seek God's calling for you today? Offer a prayer that God will open your eyes to God's presence in all situations.

Day 5:

Consider ways you feel God is calling someone you know. Perhaps you see in that person a gift for evangelism, teaching, singing, writing, etc. Use the space below to organize your thoughts and then write a letter to that person, explaining why you think God is calling him or her to a particular ministry. Sometimes all it takes for a person to answer God's call is confirmation from another person.

Day 6:

It is easy to rationalize that God uses only special people for divine purposes, but that is not the truth. We think of the calling of God as a big mission, but God might be calling us to offer a word of encouragement to someone, to express concern when someone is struggling, to be patient with a new cashier at the store, or simply to be present with a person. Think of the people with whom you regularly interact, or ones you may encounter by chance. Write down the needs you know they have. How can you help make their lives a little easier?

Day 7:

When have you wondered about the purpose for your life? How are you responding to God's call? Ask yourself what you want, then write down the answers that come to you. As you look at each answer, consider how participating in these things brings you joy. How do your actions help those around you? How does following Jesus fit into the responses? As you consider your responses to the questions, your calling may become more evident. If you continue to struggle to identify how God is calling you, ask a trusted friend to pray with you as you seek discernment.

Down by the River

Scripture for lesson: Ezekiel 1:1–2:1-7

When I was in high school and college, Monday night was always set aside to watch wrestling on television. Even though my friends and I knew that the wrestling drama was not real, we got drawn into the storyline and attached to the characters.

Most of the scenarios were very similar: Two people squared off in the ring; one was usually cast as the good guy and the other as the villain. Often after a few minutes of pushing each other around, the good guy would get the upper hand. As the action continued, I would move to the edge of my seat, totally enthralled. Then, out of nowhere, four of the bad guy's thug friends would run into the wrestling ring and pounce on the good guy. When this happened, I would scream, "That's not fair! Someone stop them!" Then, just when I thought the bad guys were going to win, the lights would go out, the music would blare, and the hero would enter the ring to save the day. For some reason, I found myself full of emotion, screaming with excitement.

Prep for the Journey

The story of Ezekiel is an example of how God moves people in unexplainable ways. In this story God picked up the prophet when he must have felt like he was being attacked from all sides.

Opinions vary as to the time in which Ezekiel lived, with some scholars placing him in the early seventh century BCE and others in the last half of the fifth century, but the text seems to place him in the first half of the sixth century. Some scholars think he was from the nation of Israel, but others argue that he was a Judean. Then there are a few who doubt that there even was such a person as Ezekiel! A lot of uncertainties surround the prophet, to say the least.

Although probably younger than Jeremiah, Ezekiel also prophesied during some of the same time. Neither prophet mentions the

How do you react to unfair situations? What gives you hope when the "bad guys" seem to be winning?

Where do you turn when you feel as if you are being attacked from all sides?

other in his writings, which was not uncommon. Scribes or disciples of the prophets probably recorded their teachings. They both proclaimed God's impending judgment on the people, and they both offered words of hope to those who were enduring God's punishment.

Ezekiel was both a prophet and a priest in Jerusalem. "If, as seems probable, Ezekiel came to Jerusalem in 591, the year following his call, he must have found the city in the midst of great tensions" *(The Interpreter's Bible, Vol. 6,* © 1956, page 58). Six years later, after an extended siege, Babylon's armies invaded and totally destroyed Jerusalem. Most of those who survived were taken captive and relocated to Babylon, where they lived in exile. One of those people was Ezekiel. The Exile continues to be seen as one of the darkest times in Israel's history.

On the Road

Ezekiel answered God's call to prophesy when he was approximately 30 years old. His call "was to proclaim the judgment of God, not to persuade to repentance" *(Ibid,* page 52). Apparently he lived in both Babylon and Jerusalem at various times during his years of prophesying.

Read Ezekiel 1:1-3.

In the thirtieth year, in the fourth month, on the fifth day of the month, as I was among the exiles by the river Chebar, the heavens were opened, and I saw visions of God. 2 On the fifth day of the month (it was the fifth year of the exile of King Jehoiachin), 3 the word of the LORD came to the priest Ezekiel son of Buzi, in the land of the Chaldeans by the river Chebar; and the hand of the LORD was on him there.

The Chebar River was probably a channel of the Euphrates River that had been diverted to provide irrigation for the area. Because a significant number of the exiles were settled in this area, they may have worked as laborers in the continued construction of this canal, or possibly others. It is also possible that the exiles had gathered by the river, which would have been away from the village, to worship. We know from references in the New Testament that when a house of worship was not available, God's people would gather by a river or outside of the town.

At the age of 30, Ezekiel should have been assuming his full priestly duties. Instead, he was laboring with others in this foreign land, unable to serve in the role for which he had been educated and trained. But God had a different purpose for Ezekiel; one that was even more important than being a priest.

How might you receive a message such as the one Ezekiel was called to proclaim?

If you did not have access to a "house of worship," how likely would you be to find a place where you could gather with others for worship?

When has God sent you in a direction other than the one for which you had prepared?

Despite all that had happened, Ezekiel continued to hope for the future of his people. God's call to become a prophet gave Ezekiel's life direction and purpose, along with a renewed hope for the future. He was then able to share that much-needed hope with the other exiles.

Much of what Ezekiel wrote is symbolic, which can make his writings difficult to understand. Due to some of his rather extreme actions (lying on one side for 390 days, on the other side for 40 days, shaving off his hair, etc), and his use of symbolic imagery, some people thought he was mentally ill.

Read Ezekiel 1:4-28.

As I looked, a stormy wind came out of the north: a great cloud with brightness around it and fire flashing forth continually, and in the middle of the fire, something like gleaming amber. ⁵ In the middle of it was something like four living creatures. This was their appearance: they were of human form. ⁶ Each had four faces, and each of them had four wings. ⁷ Their legs were straight, and the soles of their feet were like the sole of a calf's foot; and they sparkled like burnished bronze. ⁸ Under their wings on their four sides they had human hands. And the four had their faces and their wings thus: ⁹ their wings touched one another; each of them moved straight ahead, without turning as they moved. ¹⁰ As for the appearance of their faces: the four had the face of a human being, the face of a lion on the right side, the face of an ox on the left side, and the face of an eagle; ¹¹ such were their faces. Their wings were spread out above; each creature had two wings, each of which touched the wing of another, while two covered their bodies. ¹² Each moved straight ahead; wherever the spirit would go, they went, without turning as they went. ¹³ In the middle of the living creatures there was something that looked like burning coals of fire, like torches moving to and fro among the living creatures; the fire was bright, and lightning issued from the fire. ¹⁴ The living creatures darted to and fro, like a flash of lightning.

¹⁵ As I looked at the living creatures, I saw a wheel on the earth beside the living creatures, one for each of the four of them. ¹⁶ As for the appearance of the wheels and their construction: their appearance was like the gleaming of beryl; and the four had the same form, their construction being something like a wheel within a wheel. ¹⁷ When they moved, they moved in any of the four directions without veering as they moved. ¹⁸ Their rims were tall and awesome, for the rims of all four were full of eyes all around. ¹⁹ When the living creatures moved, the wheels moved beside them; and when the living creatures rose from the earth, the wheels rose. ²⁰ Wherever the spirit would go, they went, and the wheels rose along with them; for the spirit of the living creatures was in the wheels. ²¹ When they moved, the others moved; when they stopped, the others stopped; and when they rose from the earth, the wheels rose along with them; for the spirit of the living creatures was in the wheels.

²² Over the heads of the living creatures there was something like a dome, shining like crystal, spread out above their heads. ²³ Under the dome their wings were stretched out straight, one toward another; and

What gives your life hope and purpose?

How do you react to people who do odd things? How do you feel when you see a person "preaching" on a street corner or other public area?

each of the creatures had two wings covering its body. ²⁴ When they moved, I heard the sound of their wings like the sound of mighty waters, like the thunder of the Almighty, a sound of tumult like the sound of an army; when they stopped, they let down their wings. ²⁵ And there came a voice from above the dome over their heads; when they stopped, they let down their wings.

²⁶ And above the dome over their heads there was something like a throne, in appearance like sapphire; and seated above the likeness of a throne was something that seemed like a human form. ²⁷ Upward from what appeared like the loins I saw something like gleaming amber, something that looked like fire enclosed all around; and downward from what looked like the loins I saw something that looked like fire, and there was a splendor all around. ²⁸ Like the bow in a cloud on a rainy day, such was the appearance of the splendor all around. This was the appearance of the likeness of the glory of the LORD.

When I saw it, I fell on my face, and I heard the voice of someone speaking.

God really knows how to make an entrance! Ezekiel's vision began with a stormy wind coming from the north. This wind was filled with fire, light, amber, and very unusual looking creatures that combined the attributes of humans, beasts, and heavenly beings. It totally overwhelmed Ezekiel, stunning him to the point that he fell to the ground.

Most of us have very vivid dreams from time to time, ones from which we awake a little shaken. Many times those dreams don't seem to make any sense. While there can be a fine line between dreams and visions from God, there is a difference. Visions occur when a person is awake and is aware that he or she is seeing a vision; dreams occur at the end of each sleep cycle. Imagine having a dream or vision even a fraction as vivid as Ezekiel's.

Just as we are sometimes able to look back at dreams and find some meaning, modern scholars have been able to shed considerable light on the imagery in Ezekiel's vision. The beings carrying the chariot would have reminded Ezekiel of the cherubim that were on the Ark of the Covenant, which contained the Ten Commandments. Originally the Ark had resided in the Temple, which was where the people thought God was present in a special way. Without the Temple or the Ark, the people felt cut off from God. This part of the vision helped Ezekiel to know that God could not be confined to a particular place, which gave him hope that even though the Israelites were living in exile, God was still with them.

No matter how vivid our dreams or visions may be, often we cannot adequately describe them so that others can understand what we have experienced. "The brightness of God's presence seemed to Ezekiel to be like a 'bow,' or 'like a rainbow in the clouds on a rainy day.' The rainbow recalls the ancient covenant God made with humans... and extends Ezekiel's understanding of the significance of the vision" (*Ezekiel*, The Daily Bible Study Series, by Peter C. Craigie, © P.C. Craigie, 1983, pages 12-13).

When has God overwhelmed you? How did you react?

How do you react to someone who claims to have had a vision? How likely are you to believe the interpretation of a vision? Why?

Read Ezekiel 2:1-7.

He said to me: O mortal, stand up on your feet, and I will speak with you. ² And when he spoke to me, a spirit entered into me and set me on my feet; and I heard him speaking to me. ³ He said to me, Mortal, I am sending you to the people of Israel, to a nation of rebels who have rebelled against me; they and their ancestors have transgressed against me to this very day. ⁴ The descendants are impudent and stubborn. I am sending you to them, and you shall say to them, "Thus says the Lord GOD." ⁵ Whether they hear or refuse to hear (for they are a rebellious house), they shall know that there has been a prophet among them. ⁶ And you, O mortal, do not be afraid of them, and do not be afraid of their words, though briers and thorns surround you and you live among scorpions; do not be afraid of their words, and do not be dismayed at their looks, for they are a rebellious house. ⁷ You shall speak my words to them, whether they hear or refuse to hear; for they are a rebellious house.

After the big show of wild imagery, God spoke to Ezekiel, who was still lying on the ground, probably scared to death! "The vision of God that was granted to Ezekiel was not simply a profound experience, enriching the spiritual life; it was the context in which the call to service was delivered" (*Ibid*, page 14).

Ezekiel had expected to serve as a priest, which would have been his career. God's divine call for his life, though, was to be a prophet. When we respond to God's call for our life's work, it becomes our vocation rather than a career. When God calls us to a vocation, God gives us the power to undertake the task, whatever it may be. Yet, like Ezekiel, we are not promised success. Doing God's will may mean that we are surrounded by briers and thorns and live with scorpions. The assurance of God's presence gave Ezekiel the courage to continue, as it will us when we are answering God's call.

Scenic Route

The story of Ezekiel's call is different—not only in how it was delivered, but in terms of Ezekiel's response. Ezekiel was happy to see God. Before the call, he was abject, exiled in a foreign land. Just when he thought all hope was gone, God appeared.

Ezekiel had served in the Temple before being taken into captivity. It was an honor to serve in this capacity, and he probably took great pride in doing so. Ezekiel's means of serving God had been taken away from him, but God restored what he thought had been lost forever.

When has God changed the way in which you are needed to serve? How did you feel about the change?

In what situations have you felt God's presence surrounding you?

What moves you in a way you can't explain?

What does it mean to understand God with your heart instead of your head? How do we do that? In what ways does Ezekiel's story meet the definition of apocalyptic?

How have you seen God deliver calls to people today? Who do you think might be a modern-day prophet? Describe your reasoning. How can you tell the difference between a prophet called by God and a false prophet?

How do you feel about the process necessary for ordination? Why?

When we encounter scriptures like these passages from Ezekiel, we often find ourselves lost in trying to derive any meaning from them. Such passages are called apocalyptic and were assumed to make revelations of the ultimate divine purpose, with the forces of good permanently triumphing over the forces of evil (dictionary.com [December 8, 2016]). Apocalyptic stories are meant move us emotionally to a place of hope. They are to be understood with our hearts rather than our heads.

Workers Ahead — CAUTION

Ezekiel had strange visions and did odd things, but he was faithful to God. If someone today were to share the vision that Ezekiel had, we would probably assume he or she was under the influence of some kind of drug. People who claim to have had unusual visions from God today are often dismissed and even ridiculed.

We know that God continues to call people to serve and that some of those calls come in unique ways. In the Cumberland Presbyterian Church, a person who feels that God has called him or her to ordained ministry of word and sacrament must have that call validated before a presbytery will approve him or her for ordination. The validation comes in the form of an invitation to serve in an official capacity related to ministry (i.e. chaplaincy, pastor, youth minister). This type of check and balance helps guard against putting into leadership positions people who may have misunderstood God's call, people who are not suited for this type of ministry, or even who those who are false prophets.

As Ezekiel learned, God was with him and the people even in Babylon. Just as God was not contained within the Temple, God is not confined to the building where we worship. God is not limited to showing up at special places, with special people, at special times. God shows up at everyday places, with everyday people, every day. God calls each of us to share with others the hope that comes from this assurance.

In the Rear View

In a sense, we have all been down by the Chebar River. Life can beat us up. Sometimes we feel like that wrestler in the middle of the ring with five other people kicking us from every angle. We get the sense that God is nowhere to be found.

Yet, as Ezekiel learned, God is with us no matter where we are. We can feel as if we are exiled in a foreign land, but God is there. We may feel hopeless, but God is there to lift us up and give encouragement. When we are being kicked from every angle, God is with us, ready to be our personal hero and set us on a path of service that will bring fulfillment. Thanks be to God!

How would your outlook on life change if you looked for God in all situations, instead of just the ones in which you expect to find God? When have you found God in the place you least expected?

Travel Log

Day 1:

When have you felt as if you were being kicked from every side? How did God help you to find a way out of that situation? As you reflect about that time, journal your thoughts in the space below.

Day 2:

What situation in your own life could compare to the destruction of Jerusalem and the exile of her people? Make notes about how you felt during that time. Then, think of others in your life who may be experiencing their own exile. Consider how you can reach out to offer them hope.

Day 3:

Many everyday things move us spiritually without us understanding why. Jot down a few things such as songs, sights, feelings, and situations that move you deeply. Write a prayer of thanks for the presence of these things in your life.

Day 4:

There are times when the presence of God feels especially strong around us. Take a moment to consider when you have experienced such a time. Either write or draw a picture that could help you to share your experience with someone else. How are you best able to convey the richness of God's presence?

Day 5:

How do you best listen to God—with your heart or your head? Sometimes our heads hear one thing, but our hearts, which I define as the seat of our spiritual conscience, hear something different. List some ways that you think with your head (for example, 2+2=4, the sky is blue, etc.). Then list some ways you think with your heart. What is the value of each way of thinking?

Day 6:

If you were called to be a prophet in today's world, what message do you think God would give you? How would you share that message? How might you be able to prove the legitimacy of your call? What elements of hope do you think would be in the message? Write down some of your thoughts.

Day 7:

Not every person's career is his or her vocation. What is your vocation? How has it been validated? What successes and struggles have you experienced in following your vocation? Journal your thoughts.

God Can Use Me?

Scripture for lesson: Luke 5:1-11, 27-32; 6:12-16

We all do things that we shouldn't, things of which God doesn't approve. One day my youngest daughter sought me out to report, "Sister hit me."

About the same time my older daughter came out of her room protesting, "I hit her but she was getting into my stuff." My wife and I explained that there would never be a reason to hit her sister and sent her to her room.

When I went in to tell our daughter what her punishment was, she had tears in her eyes. As I sat beside her, she asked, "Is my sister okay?"

"Yes, she is fine."

"I'm so sorry; I am such a bad person."

My child was dealing with shame over a mistake she had made. Putting my arms around her, I whispered, "I love you."

She asked, "Why?"

"Because you are mine."

Prep for the Journey

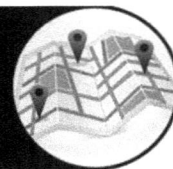

In Luke's account, Jesus was already preaching and teaching when he called his first disciples. Jesus seeking out people rather than their coming to him was not the norm. When other teachers of the time began their public ministry, students would more or less apply to be one of their disciples. If the teacher did not want that particular person as a disciple, he would give the potential follower the brush off: "You need to study the Torah more first" or "It would be best if you followed in your father's occupation." The teacher's hope was that his disciples would learn all they could from him and then become teachers with their own groups of disciples.

It's quite possible that people had already applied to be disciples of Jesus. But he had other ideas about the type of people who would be

---

Why do you love someone? Whose are you?

What do you think about the possibility that Jesus may have turned away some people who wanted to be his students/ disciples? Why might he have done so?

best suited to carry on his ministry and teachings. It is unlikely that any of the teachers of Jesus' time would have accepted as disciples the men Jesus specifically called.

On the Road

Jesus' disciples were common, working-class people. They were not well educated, nor were they at the top of the social register. In fact, they would have been rejected by many. People did not generally interact outside their social class at that time, but from the beginning of his ministry, Jesus did things differently.

Read Luke 5:1-11.

Once while Jesus was standing beside the lake of Gennesaret, and the crowd was pressing in on him to hear the word of God, ² he saw two boats there at the shore of the lake; the fishermen had gone out of them and were washing their nets. ³ He got into one of the boats, the one belonging to Simon, and asked him to put out a little way from the shore. Then he sat down and taught the crowds from the boat. ⁴ When he had finished speaking, he said to Simon, "Put out into the deep water and let down your nets for a catch." ⁵ Simon answered, "Master, we have worked all night long but have caught nothing. Yet if you say so, I will let down the nets." ⁶ When they had done this, they caught so many fish that their nets were beginning to break. ⁷ So they signaled their partners in the other boat to come and help them. And they came and filled both boats, so that they began to sink. ⁸ But when Simon Peter saw it, he fell down at Jesus' knees, saying, "Go away from me, Lord, for I am a sinful man!" ⁹ For he and all who were with him were amazed at the catch of fish that they had taken; ¹⁰ and so also were James and John, sons of Zebedee, who were partners with Simon. Then Jesus said to Simon, "Do not be afraid; from now on you will be catching people." ¹¹ When they had brought their boats to shore, they left everything and followed him.

Even though Jesus had just begun his ministry, a large crowd of people had gathered to listen to him teach. Seeing the boats that had just come in after a night of fishing, Jesus got on board one and asked the crew to take him out a short distance. From that vantage point he taught the crowd.

Having noticed that his hosts, Simon, James, and John, had not caught any fish, Jesus told Simon to take the boat into deeper water. Even though they had fished all night without any success, Simon did as Jesus said. When he dropped his nets this time, so many fish became trapped that the nets were beginning to break and the boat was in danger of sinking. Simon called his partners for help.

What does following Jesus mean to you? What would you think about a teacher who called fishermen and tax collectors to be his disciples?

When have you not succeeded despite your best efforts? What or who could have persuaded you to try again?

When has someone asked you to interrupt your work and "go back out"? How did you feel about accommodating the request?

What would influence you to the point of walking away from your livelihood to follow someone? How do you feel about people who do walk away from their jobs/careers to follow a specific person or engage in a ministry?

Luke tells us that the fishermen had been washing their nets when Jesus approached, so they probably weren't keen about going back out to do more fishing. Fishing nets at that time were often hundreds of feet long. They hung from pieces of cork or wood, which floated, and were weighted with pieces of lead or rocks so that the net would hang straight down. Long cords extended from both ends of the nets. The nets were usually stretched between two boats. The fishermen would have pulled the nets into a circle, trapping the fish. The nets were made from linen, which needed to be washed and dried after every use to keep them from deteriorating. Washing them would not have been an easy task, and time spent repairing nets or making new ones was time taken away from earning a living.

It may seem as if Jesus randomly came upon the fishermen, but Luke chapter 4 tells us that Jesus knew Simon. In fact, he had gone to Simon's house and healed his mother-in-law. So, Simon knew at least a little about Jesus. We can speculate about why Jesus went to preach by the lake and chose Simon's boat, but it would be just that—speculation. What we do know is that upon catching all the fish, Simon fell down at Jesus' feet, admitting his sinfulness. Then Jesus changed Simon's mission in life, but not his job title. Simon was still a fisherman, but instead of fishing for the usual catch, Jesus told him he would be fishing for people. Simon, James, and John immediately left everything to follow Jesus.

Read Luke 5:27-32.

After this he [Jesus] went out and saw a tax collector named Levi, sitting at the tax booth; and he said to him, "Follow me." [28] *And he got up, left everything, and followed him.*

[29] *Then Levi gave a great banquet for him in his house; and there was a large crowd of tax collectors and others sitting at the table with them.* [30] *The Pharisees and their scribes were complaining to his disciples, saying, "Why do you eat and drink with tax collectors and sinners?"* [31] *Jesus answered, "Those who are well have no need of a physician, but those who are sick;* [32] *I have come to call not the righteous but sinners to repentance."*

The IRS seems to be the brunt of many jokes in our society. While taxes are a necessary part of maintaining our government, I doubt that anyone likes to pay them. But the disdain we have about paying taxes or those who collect them pales in comparison to what the people in Jesus' time felt about tax collectors.

The Roman Empire hired local citizens to collect the taxes, which meant that they were working for the enemy. People did not always know the actual amount of taxes Rome required, so they had little choice but to pay whatever the tax collector demanded—even if the amount was often significantly more than what had been levied. Rome didn't care about the tax collectors' abuses as long as the empire received its portion. So, not only were they working for Rome, but they were cheating their own countrymen.

According to the Pharisees, tax collectors were "sinners"—those who did not follow the Law or at least the Law as the Pharisees interpreted it. Jesus, however, called Levi, a tax collector, to follow him. Levi responded by having a great banquet to which he invited his "sinner" friends so that they could meet Jesus. When the Pharisees challenged Jesus as to the moral legitimacy of dining with known sinners, Jesus responded, "I have come not to call the righteous but sinners to repentance."

The Pharisees didn't seem themselves as sinners. They followed the letter of the Law, which they thought equated to being righteous. The Pharisees made mistakes, as did those Jesus called to be his disciples, as do we. My daughter made a mistake, but she is my child and I will always love her. God claims us as children and will love us even when we make mistakes. After all, Jesus came for the sinners.

Read Luke 6:12-16.

Now during those days he went out to the mountain to pray; and he spent the night in prayer to God. ¹³ And when day came, he called his disciples and chose twelve of them, whom he also named apostles: ¹⁴ Simon, whom he named Peter, and his brother Andrew, and James, and John, and Philip, and Bartholomew, ¹⁵ and Matthew, and Thomas, and James son of Alphaeus, and Simon, who was called the Zealot, ¹⁶ and Judas son of James, and Judas Iscariot, who became a traitor.

Jesus did not make his selections impulsively. According to this scripture, Jesus spent the entire night in prayer, away from all distractions. By this time, Jesus had many disciples, but he chose 12 of them to be apostles. Some might ask what the difference is. Disciples were students or followers of a particular teacher. After studying with that teacher, they would pass along the sayings and teachings of the master. In Luke Chapter 10, Jesus sent out 70 disciples to proclaim God's kingdom in different towns. Apostles were messengers or ambassadors for the teacher who could act with full authority of the one who had sent them. When the teacher was no longer living or able, the apostles would continue to speak for the movement. So, choosing and calling 12 men who would continue to spread Jesus' message after he was gone was an extremely important decision.

Scenic Route

If I had been Jesus, I would have gone about calling followers differently than he did. I would definitely have started by looking for the smartest people I could find, especially those who had been educated in the Law of Moses. I then would have looked for those who

---

Who are some undesirable people in our society today, those who might be labeled as "sinners"?

What do you think Jesus' response to the Pharisees meant?

How do you seek discernment about an important decision? What or who has helped you discern God's call for your life?

Do you consider followers of Jesus in the church today to be disciples and apostles? If yes, how do you see them at work? Where do you see yourself in one of these roles?

What characteristics/abilities would you seek in potential disciples? Why?

Considering the men they were when Jesus called them, what do you see as the strengths of his apostles? How would those strengths have been valuable to Jesus' mission?

How would your opinion about the people with whom you interact change if you began to see each one as being loved by God? called by God?

What does it mean to you that Jesus still calls fallible people to follow him?

had resources. Financial support, even then, was necessary for itinerate teachers/preachers. Then, I would have sought out people who were respected for their honesty and wisdom. Those are the people to whom I would have turned for guidance and advice.

Yet Jesus did the opposite of what would have made sense to me. Jesus chose fishermen, a group known to be hard working but characterized by crude manners and rough speech. Scripture tells us that Simon Peter, Andrew, James, and John were fishermen. Some scholars think that four of the other disciples were also fishermen. Levi (Matthew) was a tax collector. Judas Iscariot's occupation may have been one in which he had responsibility for handling money considering that he served as the group's treasurer. These were the people with whom Jesus chose to spend his time and to whom he would entrust God's message.

Jesus knew that these men (with the exception of Judas Iscariot), had the strength and perseverance to share God's message far and wide. Had they been well educated in the Law of Moses, they likely would not have been receptive to Jesus' message. Had they been wealthy, they would probably have had trouble giving up their possessions to follow Jesus. Plus, their wealth could have made it hard for other people to relate to them. These men may not have been consulted for their wisdom, but more than likely they had a lot of common sense. When you consider Jesus' choices from those vantage points, they make a lot more sense.

Workers Ahead

Jesus called ordinary people to be his disciples. Contrary to other teachers of his time, he also welcomed women and children. All too often people think that there are prerequisites for serving God—that we have to be good enough, smart enough, etc. We need to remember that those to whom Jesus entrusted the work he had begun were the same type of people as we are. They were outsiders, common people, and sinners—but Jesus saw their potential. They allowed God to use them, which is the only way that any of us can fulfill God's call for our life. Jesus' followers only need to have a willingness to follow. Our response to Jesus' call should simply be to follow as well.

We must be careful that we do not become like the Pharisees, judging who can and cannot respond to God's call. Jesus accepts us warts and all, and God calls us to accept others with all their failings. So, what does it mean to accept others and their failings? Are we to trust without verification? I don't think so. Jesus made responsible choices after a period of discernment. I think we should follow his example. Just because we would not let a person with a history of driving while under the influence drive the church van does not mean that we should exclude such a person from the fellowship of worship and service with God's people. Each person is called to serve in some way, and it is necessary for the individual and the congregation to determine where his or her gifts can best be used.

In the Rear View

I am so glad that the people Jesus called to be his apostles were not those whom I would have chosen. Maybe he picked those who were undesirable because they knew what it was like to be mocked and told they were not good enough. Jesus teaches that God's grace is for all, that he died on the cross for all people. Who better to take that message with passion and enthusiasm than those who for the first time in their lives were accepted and loved and told they were good enough?

When you feel like you have blown it, when you feel all alone, and when you feel like you are unlovable, hear the soft voice of God say, "You are mine." Know that you are loved and that God has a purpose for you and your particular gifts.

How are your congregation's leaders chosen? How are the members' gifts considered when assessing leadership needs? What type of discernment process is used?

Travel Log

Day 1:

What have you done that made you feel separated from God? How did your actions keep you from using your gifts? What enabled you to move past those feelings? Journal your thoughts below.

Day 2:

Reflect about accepting God's call in your life. How you have grown in your relationship with Jesus since that time? What have you learned? How has the meaning of following Jesus changed during that time? Journal your thoughts below.

Day 3:

If someone were to ask you what it's like to follow Jesus, what would you say? Jot down some of your thoughts. As a disciple of Jesus, keep that story in your heart, ready to share with others when the opportunity arises.

Day 4:

How do you see your role in the church? What gifts do you have? Write down a few gifts that you believe you can offer your church that you might be hesitating to use. Pray for direction on how to move forward and offer your gifts to your church.

Day 5:

The job of disciples is to demonstrate God's love in the world. In what ways do you or your church spread the good news of Jesus Christ? List the ministries in which you participate that help spread the message of Jesus. What new ideas do you have that you would like to see your church implement? Share your thoughts with the session and/or your pastor.

Day 6:

Has someone ever confessed to you that he or she feels outside of God's love and forgiveness? What are some of the reasons people tend to believe that they cannot be forgiven when Jesus preaches the opposite? Write down some of the reasons people think they are beyond forgiveness. Who tells them this, and why do they think it? What is your response to people who feel this way?

Day 7:

How does it feel to know that God loves you simply because you are God's child? How does it make you feel to know that God's unconditional love and forgiveness are always available to you? Write a short prayer to thank God for never giving you what you deserve.

Living in God Every Day

Scripture for lesson: Luke 14:12-24

L
FAITH
F
E

One evening my wife and I met some friends for dinner and conversation. Two hours later, as we were getting ready to leave, I asked our server for our check. She explained that our friends had paid for our meal. "No! You shouldn't have done that," we told our friends. Our feelings were not so much ones of thankfulness, but of indebtedness.

On the way home I told my wife we needed to go out to dinner with our friends again so we could repay their generosity by treating them to a meal. A few days later we talked with our friends and again thanked them for dinner and expressed what a wonderful time we had together. I then said, "We need to do it again soon so we can pay you back."

Our friends asked, "Do you think that is why we bought you dinner, so that you would owe us? We did it because we wanted to and expect nothing in return."

Prep for the Journey

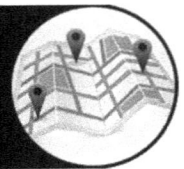

Jesus had been invited to dinner at the house of a Pharisee. In the New Testament world, meals were a social event and often lasted for several hours. They also provided an opportunity for groups of people to work out their differences.

This particular meal was held on the sabbath. Sabbath meals were usually more like celebrations or banquets. Wait a minute, you may be thinking. How could they have had this dinner on the sabbath? Wasn't any type of work forbidden on that day? No sabbath laws were broken because the food was prepared the day before and kept warm for the dinner.

Prior to the passages being considered in this lesson, Jesus had healed a man on the sabbath, which was a problem in the eyes of the

---

How do you feel when you receive an unexpected gift?

What role do meals have in your church's culture?

Pharisees. Healing was considered work, which meant that Jesus had broken the Law. The Pharisee and his guests were aware of Jesus' "sin," so they were watching and listening closely to him, hoping to find other faults.

On the Road

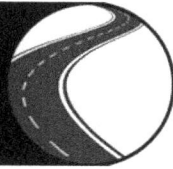

Through information included in the Gospels, we know that Jesus and the Pharisees did not see eye to eye. Perhaps Jesus' invitation to attend the Pharisee's dinner party was meant to provide an opportunity for them to sit down to discuss their differences. Whatever the intent, Jesus did not improve the Pharisees' opinion of him as he criticized the host.

Upon entering the Pharisee's house, one of the first things Jesus noticed was how the guests were jockeying for the more important seats, those closest to the host. Those guests were socially ambitious, hoping to use the invitation to further themselves. It could also be that the host was hoping to increase his social standing by inviting certain guests. Jesus used their actions to teach an important concept.

Read Luke 14:12-14.

He [Jesus] said also to the one who had invited him, "When you give a luncheon or a dinner, do not invite your friends or your brothers or your relatives or rich neighbors, in case they may invite you in return, and you would be repaid. ¹³ But when you give a banquet, invite the poor, the crippled, the lame, and the blind. ¹⁴ And you will be blessed, because they cannot repay you, for you will be repaid at the resurrection of the righteous."

As was often the case, Jesus' teaching went against the norms of society. After all, don't most people invite their friends and family when they have a special meal? So, why did Jesus say not to invite friends, family, and neighbors to dine with you?

Jesus didn't have an aversion to including those who are important to us, but he wanted to raise awareness that we are also called to invite those who have no way of repaying the kindness. At this point Jesus was challenging the condition of his listeners' hearts. Giving to others should not be a negotiating tool for something you might want in the future. According to Jesus, we should give without expecting anything in return.

Read Luke 14:15.

One of the dinner guests, on hearing this, said to him, "Blessed is anyone who will eat bread in the kingdom of God!"

Where do you see social ambition at play in today's world? How do you feel about people who are socially ambitious? Why?

When have you been invited to move to a position of greater honor or respect? How did you feel? How do you think the person whom you replaced felt?

What are some ways you can give, knowing you will not get anything in return?

What are your expectations when you give a gift to someone? Why? When have you received a gift to which expectations were tied? How did you feel about accepting the gift?

How do you envision the kingdom of God apart from life on earth? What glimpses of God's kingdom have you seen in your life?

What excuses have people given when you invited them to church? What excuses have you used for not attending church?

Whom might God be calling us to seek out and invite to join in the celebration? Where can you find these people?

In the first 13 chapters of Luke, Jesus talked a lot about the kingdom of God. Those at the dinner would have heard some of his comments. The speaker in Luke 14:15 may have been talking about what a feast would be like in God's kingdom. He was probably also thinking, *What a prestigious event that will be. I wonder how I can get an invitation!* Jesus went on to tell a parable to help his listeners understand what that party will be like.

Read Luke 14:16-24.

Then Jesus said to him, "Someone gave a great dinner and invited many. ¹⁷ At the time for the dinner he sent his slave to say to those who had been invited, 'Come; for everything is ready now.' ¹⁸ But they all alike began to make excuses. The first said to him, 'I have bought a piece of land, and I must go out and see it; please accept my regrets.' ¹⁹ Another said, 'I have bought five yoke of oxen, and I am going to try them out; please accept my regrets.' ²⁰ Another said, 'I have just been married, and therefore I cannot come.' ²¹ So the slave returned and reported this to his master. Then the owner of the house became angry and said to his slave, 'Go out at once into the streets and lanes of the town and bring in the poor, the crippled, the blind, and the lame.' ²² And the slave said, 'Sir, what you ordered has been done, and there is still room.' ²³ Then the master said to the slave, 'Go out into the roads and lanes, and compel people to come in, so that my house may be filled. ²⁴ For I tell you, none of those who were invited will taste my dinner.'"

Everything was ready for the party; the only thing missing was the guests. Keep in mind that these guests had been invited previously, and the servant was simply sent to notify them that everything was ready, that it was time for the party to begin. Jesus told about three people who declined the invitation. On the surface, their excuses seemed pretty legitimate. One had just purchased some land, one had recently purchased five yoke of oxen, and the third had recently gotten married.

The servant reported the guests' excuses to his master, who was furious. So, he sent the servant out to invite people other than his friends, relatives, and neighbors—people who could not repay the invitation. When there was still room at the feast, the master sent the servant out to search for even more people.

Scenic Route

The excuses offered by the invited guests in this story were flimsy, at best. Who purchases land without first looking at it? My wife and I bought a house 8 years ago. We looked at that house at least a dozen times before deciding to buy it. I don't know anyone who would make a purchase like this sight unseen.

The second person's excuse was that he had purchased 5 yoke of oxen and he needed to try them out. Growing up on a farm, we never bought farm equipment without finding out if it worked well. Yet this person bought 5 yoke of oxen before making sure they were healthy and worked well together.

The third person really seems to have had the best excuse. We can understand someone who had recently been married taking a rain check on an invitation. But when you look at things from that cultural perspective, this excuse was suspect as well. According to ancient Jewish law, a newly married man was excused from business and military duties for a year after the marriage. So, a newly married man would have had plenty of free time to attend the celebration.

Some people refer to excuses as "plausible lies." They are ways in which people rationalize what they want to do. The invited guests may have thought the celebration would be dull and boring; their own pursuits definitely held more interest than such an event. However, what they were so quick to refuse was quickly accepted by others—people whom the invited guests would have considered to be the dregs of society.

The guests invited to the banquet would have been of a similar financial and social status as the host. That he could afford to give a banquet for so many people tells us that he was a man of means. To have been able to purchase five yoke of oxen or a piece of property also implied wealth. When people think they are doing well on their own, they tend to push God away. Often it is only when we experience difficulty that we turn to God.

Jesus was trying to help the Pharisees and other Jews see themselves in this parable. God was calling them to a banquet beyond anything they had ever experienced, but they were refusing the invitation. They were more concerned with maintaining the status quo than mixing with undesirables. God calls all of us to accept the invitation to this banquet.

Workers Ahead

This series of lessons focuses on God's call. The previous lessons have dealt with God's call on a particular person's life, but this lesson helps us to understand that we are each called to bring in all those who will come. There is always room for another guest at God's banquet table.

What actions do you rationalize? Why?

Why is it we tend to reach out to God more often when we need help? What are some disciplines we can participate in everyday to keep us connected to God?

How are you responding to God's invitation to the banquet?

How are you inviting people to join God's banquet? What excuses have you given for not inviting more people?

How can you answer God's call in a way that will help more people respond to the banquet invitation? Make a list of some of the possibilities.

How can you be more welcoming to all of God's people? How can your congregation be more welcoming?

As a group, identify those in your community who would be the people in the streets and lanes, those who are poor, crippled, blind, and lame. If you called them to join you at God's banquet, how likely would they be to come?

Answering God's call means leaving the safety and security of our world to meet people where they are. So many of our churches have the mentality that those on the outside know where the church is located and when services are so they will come if they want to. But many people, even those who may look and act like us, don't feel welcome in God's house. Maybe they know very little about the Bible and are afraid they will feel humiliated if someone asks them a question. Maybe they don't speak clearly and have previously been asked to read aloud at a church. What if they are unfamiliar with the rituals observed in worship (i.e. automatically standing when singing the "Doxology")? Think about other concerns of people who have not shared your cultural and religious experiences.

In the Rear View

The scripture used in this lesson has many layers. It is directed to the hearts of all humans. God issues an invitation for everyone to participate in the Kingdom. Jesus' teachings help us to understand that we are called to welcome all people to God's banquet—not just those who look like us, have clean clothing, smell nice, or who were born into Christian homes.

Jesus' parable sets the standard for us. How will you respond?

Travel Log

Day 1:

Recall the unexpected gifts you have received and the joy that came from those gifts. Then consider how you can give someone else an unexpected gift. Maybe when at a drive-thru restaurant, you could pay for the order of the person behind you. Maybe you could write a letter to someone, telling how much you appreciate the gifts he or she shares. Invite someone to your home for a meal. To whom is God calling you to give an unexpected gift? Make some notes below about the possibilities and how you will act upon them.

Day 2:

Climbing the social ladder is just as prevalent today as in Jesus' time—maybe more so. Why do you think people feel the need to improve their image or status by associating with "the right people"? When have you adopted this mindset? Maybe you didn't want your child to be friends with a certain family, or you wanted your child to attend a prestigious school. As you reflect on any personal instances of social ambition, write a prayer asking God for forgiveness for those you overlooked as a result of that ambition.

Day 3:

In what situations are you more likely to turn to God—when things are going well or when you are struggling? Why do you think people tend to turn to God more when they are experiencing difficulties? Be very honest with yourself in listing the times when you have turned to God within the past couple of weeks. Write down the words help and thanksgiving/praise. Under each word list things about which you want to pray and then lift them up to God.

Day 4:

If you have ever given a party, you know how difficult it is to get people to RSVP to invitations. Even when the host includes a stamped and pre-addressed return envelope, many people still don't respond. Sometimes even when people have responded that they plan to attend, they decide at the last minute not to come. When has something similar happened to you or to a close friend or family member? How did you feel? How did you deal with the disappointment, resentment, adjusting plans, etc? Journal about your thoughts and feelings.

Day 5:

Take time to ponder how you can welcome to God's banquet people who are outside your regular circle of friends and family. What perceptions do you need to change? How willing are you to develop relationships with people who are different from you? How might you be able to develop relationships with such people? Jot down some ideas in the space below.

Day 6:

How might you be more welcoming to people who respond to God's invitation to the banquet? What expectations do you have of those who accept this gift? What expectations does God have of them? of you? of your congregation? Write down some of your thoughts and periodically review them.

Day 7:

The next time you plan a party, invite someone whom you would not ordinarily include. Maybe this person is someone with whom you have never seemed to find anything in common or someone with whom you have had a long-standing disagreement. Maybe it could be someone you met at the laundromat or while standing in line for a food order, etc. What are you willing to risk as you answer God's call? Journal your thoughts below.

Nothing Can Separate Us

Scripture for lesson: Acts 9:1-19

L
FAITH
I
F
E

One Saturday afternoon my family and I were enjoying a lazy day at home. Our daughters, who are 11, 9, and 3, were playing in their room while my wife and I watched television. When it sounded as if our daughters were getting a little rowdy, I went in their room to find them practicing dance moves. I cautioned the older two girls to be careful around their younger sister.

It wasn't long until we heard a thump and a scream. Our 3-year-old daughter came running into the living room, tears running down her face. The older two girls had been doing cartwheels, but when the youngest tried to do one, she landed on her head. I noticed that my wife was almost in tears as she tried to comfort our child. It was as if she were also feeling the pain of the bumped head. She didn't feel for our daughter, but with her. As parents, when our children hurt, we hurt. Jesus said that what we do to members of his family we do to him.

Prep for the Journey

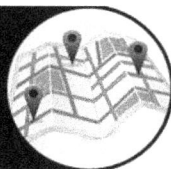

The Book of Acts is the second half of the Gospel of Luke. While some people may think that Luke was one of Jesus' close followers, he was actually a Gentile convert who traveled with Paul. Luke was an educated man, evidenced by his writing style; Paul referred to him as a physician. Probably because he was a Gentile, Luke's Gospel and Acts are addressed more to that population rather than to the Jews. Luke wanted people to know that the gospel was meant for everyone, not just the chosen few.

The message of Jesus was spreading far and wide thanks to Jesus' apostles and those who had become believers after his resurrection. In the beginning it was thought to be only a sect developing within the Jewish faith. Because so many of Jesus' teachings challenged the

> Often when people we love hurt, we hurt, and when they experience joy, we are joyful. Who are those people in your life and what examples can you recall of feeling their joy or pain?

> How might your attitude cause others to believe that the gospel message was not meant for them?

How might growth be limited by a church being in "protection mode"? How can Christians be sure that any movement or growth is of God?

What causes a person to become zealous? About what do you feel zealous? Why?

Where is the church today finding itself in opposition to the law of the land?

Where do you see the persecution of Christians today?

When have you thought you were doing something good and righteous only to discover that your actions were in opposition to what was truly right?

traditional views of the Jewish religious leaders, many of those leaders openly opposed the disciples' efforts. They were trying to protect what they felt to be the truth.

The tension between the two groups came to a head when Stephen, a follower of Jesus, was stoned for challenging the Jewish establishment, basing his statements on the teachings of Jesus. Luke tells us that a young man named Saul watched these proceedings and approved of the group's actions. He even watched over their cloaks while they stoned Stephen.

Saul had grown up in Jewish home, which meant that he would have been well instructed in the traditions and scriptures. As a young adult, Saul went to Jerusalem, where he trained under the best teacher of the time, Gamaliel. Saul became very zealous in his beliefs, which stemmed from the laws and traditions of the Old Testament.

Saul was a Pharisee. This group controlled the synagogues and held a lot of control over the general Jewish population. Pharisees separated themselves to study and interpret the law. Teaching against the laws of the Old Testament was considered blasphemy. Jesus and Stephen were both accused of blasphemy, which justified their deaths to those in power. After Stephen's death, the followers of Jesus scattered throughout the Roman Empire, taking the gospel with them.

On the Road

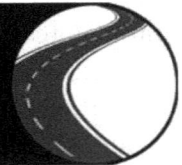

Filled with zealous enthusiasm, Saul was determined to stop the spread of Christianity. With the approval of the high priest, Saul personally sought out the followers of Jesus. If you were a follower of Jesus, the mention of the Saul's name would have brought fear.

Read Acts 9:1-2.

Meanwhile Saul, still breathing threats and murder against the disciples of the Lord, went to the high priest [2] and asked him for letters to the synagogues at Damascus, so that if he found any who belonged to the Way, men or women, he might bring them bound to Jerusalem.

Saul took seriously his mission of rounding up the followers of "The Way." He felt that the world needed to be rid of this group of people who proclaimed Jesus as Messiah. Hearing that a group of followers had settled in Damascus, Saul and his contingent headed for that city, determined to find any of these heretics and bring them to justice. Saul would have considered imprisonment or death as a fitting form of justice in this instance.

Read Acts 9:3-9.

Now as he [Saul] was going along and approaching Damascus, suddenly a light from heaven flashed around him. ⁴ He fell to the ground and heard a voice saying to him, "Saul, Saul, why do you persecute me?" ⁵ He asked, "Who are you, Lord?" The reply came, "I am Jesus, whom you are persecuting. ⁶ But get up and enter the city, and you will be told what you are to do." ⁷ The men who were traveling with him stood speechless because they heard the voice but saw no one. ⁸ Saul got up from the ground, and though his eyes were open, he could see nothing; so they led him by the hand and brought him into Damascus. ⁹ For three days he was without sight, and neither ate nor drank.

As Saul approached Damascus, a powerful light flashed around him, blinding him. Those who were with Saul could not see anything, but they could hear the voice that spoke to Saul. Saul was so convinced that he was doing the right thing by persecuting the Christians that it took this act to get his attention.

He discovered that the one whose followers he had been persecuting was actually the one true God. How confused Saul must have felt—and how guilty. Saul thought he was doing God's will by silencing the blasphemous heretics. Saul discovered instead that he was actually hindering God and God's work.

God's call humbled the arrogant young Saul. His traveling companions had to lead him into Damascus, where he remained blind for three days. During that time, Saul probably spent a lot of time in prayer and contemplation. After all, it's not every day one has such a dramatic encounter with Jesus.

Read Acts 9:10-19.

Now there was a disciple in Damascus named Ananias. The Lord said to him in a vision, "Ananias." He answered, "Here I am, Lord." ¹¹ The Lord said to him, "Get up and go to the street called Straight, and at the house of Judas look for a man of Tarsus named Saul. At this moment he is praying, ¹² and he has seen in a vision a man named Ananias come in and lay his hands on him so that he might regain his sight." ¹³ But Ananias answered, "Lord, I have heard from many about this man, how much evil he has done to your saints in Jerusalem; ¹⁴ and here he has authority from the chief priests to bind all who invoke your name." ¹⁵ But the Lord said to him, "Go, for he is an instrument whom I have chosen to bring my name before Gentiles and kings and before the people of Israel; ¹⁶ I myself will show him how much he must suffer for the sake of my name." ¹⁷ So Ananias went and entered the house. He laid his hands on Saul and said, "Brother Saul, the Lord Jesus, who appeared to you on your way here, has sent me so that you may regain your sight and be filled with the Holy Spirit." ¹⁸ And immediately something like scales fell from his eyes, and his sight was restored. Then he got up and was baptized, ¹⁹ and after taking some food, he regained his strength.

For several days he was with the disciples in Damascus.

When have you had to forgive someone who terribly offended you? What did that feel like?

When have you felt unworthy of God's love? When have you had difficulty forgiving yourself?

To whom would you have trouble offering God's love? Why?

For ages this story has been known as the "Call of Saul," but it could easily be titled the "Call of Ananias." Saul's evil ways were so well known that when God called Ananias to heal Saul, Ananias was hesitant. Who can blame him? How might one of us have responded if God had called us to go to Adolf Hitler, Jeffrey Dahmer, or the hijackers responsible for the terrorist attacks of September 11? I think most of us would have taken a pass. Yet, Ananias followed the call of God. He placed his hands on Saul and Saul's sight was restored. Ananias then baptized the man whom he once feared so greatly.

After spending time with the disciples in Damascus, Saul became as zealous, maybe even more so, about spreading the gospel than he had been about trying to stop it. Saul, who was also known by his Roman name of Paul, began a journey that was often difficult and dangerous, but he became one of the most important voices for Jesus, and the Lord became his passion.

Scenic Route

Jesus asked Saul an interesting question: "Saul, Saul, why do you persecute me?" Saul was actually persecuting the followers of Jesus, not Jesus himself. We might expect Jesus to ask: "Saul, why do you persecute my followers?" but he didn't, which gives us some insight into the nature of Jesus and of God.

When we hurt, God hurts. Jesus is just like that mother who felt the pain of her daughter when she bumped her head while trying to do cartwheels. God does not sit in heaven and watch, but rather God is involved in our lives. God will hold those who hurt and actually enter into their pain with them. When we wonder whether or not God cares, we need to remember that God is with us in our hurt and pain, our joys and sorrows. The next time we hurt and cry out, "Where are you, God?" the answer is, "I'm beside you, crying as well."

How does it make you feel to know that Jesus and God experience your pain and joy?

Workers Ahead

For millennia people have been justifying actions by doing them in God's name or for God's kingdom. Consider The Inquisition, during which people could level charges of heresy and the one under question was allowed no rights, usually found guilty, and sometimes

66

burned at the stake. At that point, heresy usually involved having a view of religion different from that of the Catholic Church, which was the primary church at the time.

The Holocaust came after centuries of anti-Semitism, which was fueled by Christians. Despite news reports about thousands of Jews being killed, people throughout Europe, including religious leaders, turned a blind eye and a deaf ear. People in other parts of the world did no better.

The Ku Klux Klan claims to be a Christian organization. In the Klan's heyday during the 1920s, many of its members were also anti-Semitic and anti-Catholic. The Klan continues to be active today.

Throughout the history of the United States, people have used religion as a basis for all sorts of evil, including witch trials, discrimination, and segregation. Unfortunately, some of these evils continue today, and people continue to justify their actions by referencing the Bible or religious viewpoints.

God calls us to seek the fair treatment of all people. Jesus died for all of God's people, so why shouldn't we treat them with love and respect?

This story of Saul/Paul is one of the greatest stories of how God can take someone whose life is disgusting and evil and turn it into something beautiful. If there is hope for the person who made it his personal mission to wipe out Christianity, God can still make something beautiful out of the mess of our lives. In Paul's letter to the Romans, he said, "God proves his love for us in that while we still were sinners Christ died for us" (5:8). Christ didn't die for us once we become good people. Christ didn't die for us once we figured out everything. Christ died for us in our confusion, doubt, selfishness, greed and all other types of sinfulness that creep into our lives.

Jesus met Saul in all his evil and sinfulness and offered forgiveness and hope. That same hope and forgiveness is available to all of us. No matter what we do, God can and will forgive us.

In the Rear View

Over the past few weeks we have explored instances of God's call on the lives of people. In several of the examples, God told the person the purpose for his life. We may wonder why God doesn't seem to speak directly to us today. Wouldn't it be nice if God would just speak to us loud and clear in the same way it seems to happen in the Bible? Couldn't God come to us in the form of a burning bush to get our attention like Moses or just blind us with a light like Jesus did to Paul to let us know the direction we need to journey? I believe God still does!

In what situations do you see the Church—or religion—promoting unjust treatment of people? What is God calling you to do about the situation?

How can you remind yourself of God's unconditional love and forgiveness when you feel unworthy?

What do you think of the statement, "Why doesn't God speak to us the way God did to people in the Bible?"

What are some distractions that might prevent you from hearing God?

However, there are two things that get in the way of us hearing God's voice. First, the direction that God knows is best for our life might not be the direction that we want to follow. Many times our prayers involve us wanting God to validate our desires. If we have learned anything from the stories of calling, most people who hear and listen to God's direction for their lives see it as a disruption of their plans. For us to hear God, we need to empty ourselves of our own plans and desires.

Second, the world in which we live has more distractions than at any time in the history of the world. Maybe one reason we can't hear God is because there is so much other noise around us. Now more than ever, we need to take time to be quiet and to listen. We all know the importance of praying, but it is just as important to take time to listen. If we ask God to lead us and give us direction but then pick up the remote to watch television, how can we ever expect to hear clarity from God? In this world of loud noises and chaos, quiet yourself and simply listen. You might be surprised at what you hear.

Travel Log

Day 1:

Most humans have an inherent desire to do good things, but sometimes our efforts become entangled and distorted, causing us to do harm rather than good. Maybe we supported a political candidate who kept his or her real agenda hidden until after the election. Maybe you gave someone a positive reference without knowing his or her complete history. There are also times when we come to a different understanding about an issue, which causes us to change our focus and efforts.

Think about times when you have done harm when you thought you were doing something good. Write down some thoughts about how you felt upon realizing what you had done. How were you able to reconcile these feelings and experience God's grace?

Day 2:

Saul did not do anything halfway, but approached with zeal the things about which he felt passionate. What do you approach with zeal? Why? Where do you wish you felt more zeal? Journal your thoughts about these questions.

Day 3:

Think of a situation in which you have had a tough time forgiving someone. What feelings did you experience toward that person? How did you feel once you were able forgive him or her? If you haven't been able to forgive that person, how are your feelings affecting your life? Write a prayer asking God to intervene in your heart so that you are able to forgive. Then try to write a letter to the person whom you have been able to forgive.

Day 4:

Just like there have been times when we need to forgive others, there are also times when we need forgiveness. When have you sought forgiveness only to be denied? Journal about your feelings in that situation. Know that even though others may hold a grudge, God has forgiven you. Pray for God's reconciliation.

Day 5:

God's call in our lives can be disruptive, which usually makes us uncomfortable. In what ways do you feel God might be calling you? How would answering that call take you out of your comfort zone? What are your hesitancies about responding to God's call? List your fears and/or concerns about accepting this call. Ask God to ease your fears.

Day 6:

Find a place free of distractions, one in which you can be guaranteed some uninterrupted time. As you sit in silence for at least five minutes, focus on listening for God. Make notes about any impressions or thoughts that come to mind during this time. As you reflect on your notes, consider what God might be saying to you.

Day 7:

Jesus calls the Church to follow the Spirit of God in new and exciting ways. In what ways have you noticed that your church has become stagnant? In what ways has it resisted change and held onto doing things the same way? Write down some ways you feel the Spirit is leading your church and the directions you feel it should go. Share your thoughts and feelings with the church session or your pastor.

www.ingramcontent.com/pod-product-compliance
Lightning Source LLC
Chambersburg PA
CBHW081151040426
42445CB00015B/1842